LINCOLNSHIRE
Wit & Humour

DONNA NOOK

BRADWELL
BOOKS

Published by Bradwell Books

9 Orgreave Close Sheffield S13 9NP

Email: books@bradwellbooks.co.uk

Compiled by Donna Nook

British Library Cataloguing in Publication Data: a catalogue record for
this book is available from the British Library.

1st Edition

ISBN: 9781909914674

Print: Gomer Press, Llandysul, Ceredigion SA44 4JL

Design by: jenksdesign@yahoo.co.uk/07506 471162

Illustrations: ©Tim O'Brien 2014

A teacher at a school in Gainsborough was having a little trouble getting her Year 11 pupils to understand grammar. "These are what we call the pronouns," she said, "We use them with verbs like this: I am, you are, he/she is." The pupils looked at her with glazed expressions.

Trying a different tack, she said, "Lauren, give me a sentence with the pronoun, 'I' in it."

Lauren began, "I is..."

"No, no, no, no, no NO, NO!" shouted the teacher, "Never, 'I is', always, 'I am'... now try again."

Lauren looked puzzled and a little hurt, thought a while then began again more quietly, "I... am... the ninth letter of the alphabet."

Two elderly ladies in Withernsea had been friends for many decades. Over the years, they had shared all kinds of fun but of late as dementia started to take its toll their activities had been limited to meeting a few times a week to play cards. One day, they were playing pontoon when one looked at the other and said, "Now don't get mad at me, duck. I know we've been friends for a long time but I just can't think of your name. I've thought and thought, but I can't remember it. Please tell me what your name is." Her friend got a bit mardy and, for at least three minutes, she just stared and glared at her. Finally she said, "How soon do you need to know?"

The magistrate at Lincoln County Court spoke sharply to the defendant, "But if you saw the lady driving towards you, why didn't you give her half the road?"

"I was going to, your Honour," replied the motorist, "…as soon as I could work out which half she wanted."

Two rival cricketers from Cuxwold and Bassingham were having a chat.

"The local team wants me to play for them very badly," said the man from Cuxwold."

"Well," said his friend, "You're just the man for the job."

Patient: "Doctor, doctor! I think I need glasses."

Man: "You certainly do, this is a pet shop. "

A man goes to the doctor with a strawberry growing out of his head. The Doc says, "I'll give you some cream to put on it."

Simon was down on his luck so he thought he would try getting a few odd jobs by calling at the posh houses in Grantham. After a few "no ways", a guy in one of the big houses thought he would give him a break and said, "The porch needs painting so I'll give you £50 to paint it for me."

"You're life-saver, mister," says Simon, "I'll get started right away!"

Time passes until…

"There you go, I'm all done with the painting."

"Well, here's your £50," says the homeowner, handing over some crisp tenners.

"Thanks very much," says Simon, pocketing the money, "Oh and by the way, it's a Ferrari, not a Porsche!"

Just before the big race at Market Rasen, the trainer was giving last minute instructions to the jockey and appeared to slip something into the horse's mouth just as a steward walked by.

"What was that?" inquired the steward.

"Oh nothing," said the trainer, "just a polo."

He offered one to the steward and had one himself. After the suspicious steward had left the scene, the trainer continued with his instructions.

"Just keep on the rail. You're on a dead cert. The only thing that could possibly pass you down the home straight is either the steward or me."

Q: What's the difference between a lawyer and a vampire?

A: A vampire only sucks blood at night.

Insurance Assessor: "What gear were you in at the moment of the impact?"

Woman Driver: "Gucci sweats and Reeboks."

"Dad," says the little boy," Can I play football with the lads in the street?"

"No,"says his dad,"They swear too much."

"But you play with them, Dad?"

"I swear already."

A rather cocky young man, who worked on a busy construction site in Lincoln, was bragging that he could outdo anyone in a feat of strength. He made a special case of making fun of Morris, one of the more senior workmen. After several minutes, Morris had had enough.

"Why don't you put your money where your mouth is?" he said. "I'll bet a week's wages that I can haul something in a wheelbarrow over to that outbuilding that you won't be able to wheel back again."

"You're on, mate," the cocky young man replied. "It's a bet! Let's see what you got."

Morris reached out and grabbed the wheelbarrow by the handles. Then, nodding to the young man, he said, "All right. Get in."

Fred's wife has been missing for over a week. The police liaison officer warned him to prepare for the worst…so Fred went to the charity shop to get all her clothes back.

A lad from Grimsby who had just started his first term at De Montfort University, Leicester, asked a third year, "Can you tell me where the library's at?"

The older student said disdainfully, "At De Montfort, we never end a sentence with a preposition."

The new boy tried again, "Can you tell me where the library's at, you wally?"

A lawyer from Leicester and a businessman from Lincoln ended up sitting next to each other on a long-haul flight.

The lawyer started thinking that he could have some fun at the man from Lincoln's expense and asked him if he'd like to play a fun game. The businessman was tired and just wanted to relax. He politely declined the offer and tried to sleep. The lawyer persisted, explaining, "I ask you a question, and if you don't know the answer, you pay me just £5; you ask me one, and if I don't know the answer, I will pay you £500."

This got the businessman a little more interested and he finally agreed to play the game.

The lawyer asked the first question, "What's the distance from the Earth to the moon?"

The man from Lincoln said nothing, but reached into his pocket, pulled out a five-pound note and handed it to the lawyer.

Now, it was his turn to ask a question. He asked the lawyer, "What goes up a hill with three legs, and comes down with four?"

The lawyer scratched his head. He looked the question up on his laptop and searched the web. He sent emails to his most well-read friends. He used the air-phone to call his colleagues in Leicester, but he still came up with nothing. After over an hour of searching, he finally gave up.

He woke up the businessman and handed him £500. The man pocketed the cash smugly and dozed off again.

The lawyer was wild with curiosity and wanted to know the answer. He shook the businessman awake. "Well? What goes up a hill with three legs and comes down with four?" he demanded.

The businessman reached into his pocket, handed the lawyer £5 and went straight back to sleep.

An elderly couple from Heckington are sitting at the dining table in their semi-detached house talking about making preparations for writing their wills. Bill says to his missus, Edna, "I've been thinking, my dear, if I go first to meet me maker I don't want you to be on your own for too long. In fact, I think you could do worse than marry Colin in the Chemists or Dave with the fruit stall in the market. They'd provide for you and look after you when I'm gone."

"That's very kind on you to think about me like that, Bill," replied Edna, "But I've already made my own arrangements!"

Two elderly ladies were enjoying a small sherry in their local in Spilsby.

One said to the other, "Was it love at first sight when you met your late husband?"

"No, I don't think so," came the reply, "I didn't know how much money he had when I first met him!"

Why was the computer so tired when it got home?

Because it had a hard drive!

A man from Waddington said to his wife, "Get your coat on love. I'm off to the club."

His wife said, "That's nice. You haven't taken me out for years."

He said, "You're not coming with me...I'm turning the heating off when I go out."

A bloke from Humberston goes into an artist's studio and asks if the artist could paint a picture of him surrounded by beautiful, scantily clad women. The artist agrees but he is intrigued by this strange request. He asks his new client why he wants such a picture painted and the bloke says, "Well, if I die before me missus when she finds this painting she'll wonder which one I spent all me money on!"

The next day the bloke's wife goes into the artist's studio and asks him to paint her wearing a big diamond necklace and matching earrings.

"Of course, madam," says the artist, "but may I ask why?"

"Well," replies the woman, "if I die before me husband I want his new woman to be frantic searching for all me jewellery!"

Derek and Duncan were long-time neighbours in Sutton-on-Sea. Every time, Derek saw Duncan coming round to his house, his heart sank. This was because he knew that, as always, Duncan would be visiting him in order to borrow something and he was fed up with it.

"I'm not going to let Duncan get away with it this time," he said quietly to his wife, "Watch what I'm about to do."

"Hi there, I wondered if you were thinking about using your hedge trimmer this afternoon?" asked Duncan.

"Oh, I'm very sorry," said Derek, trying to look apologetic, "but I'm actually going to be using it all afternoon."

"In that case," replied Duncan with a big grin, "You won't be using your golf clubs, will you? Mind if I borrow them?"

Light travels faster than sound. That's why some people appear bright until you hear them speak.

A Lincolnshire man is driving through Leicestershire, when he passes a farmer standing in the middle of a huge field. He pulls the car over and watches the farmer standing stock-still, doing absolutely nothing. Intrigued, the man walks over to the farmer and asks him, "Excuse me sir, but what are you doing?"

The farmer replies, "I'm trying to win a Nobel Prize."

"How?" Asks the puzzled Lincolnshire man.

"Well," says the farmer, "I heard they give the prize to people who are outstanding in their field."

A well-known academic from the University of Leicester was giving a lecture on the philosophy of language at the University of Lincoln. He came to a curious aspect of English grammar.

"You will note," said the somewhat stuffy scholar, "That in the English language, two negatives can mean a positive, but it is never the case that two positives can mean a negative."

To which someone at the back responded, "Yeah, yeah."

What do you call the two people that always have to embarrass you the most in front of all your friends? Mum and Dad.

A police officer was patrolling the lanes outside Spalding one night, when he noticed a car swerving all over the road. Quickly, he turned on his lights and siren and pulled the driver over. "Sir, do you know you're all over the road? Please step out of the car."

When the man got out of the car, the policeman told him to walk in a straight line.

"I'd be happy to, offisher," said the drunk, "If you can just get the line to stop moving about."

Why is a clock like a depressed person? It's forever running itself down!

A rabbit went to the fortune-teller.

"What do you see in my future?" asked the rabbit.

"Very soon," replied the fortune-teller, "you will meet a pretty young girl who will want to know everything about you, inside and out."

"That's great!" said the rabbit, hopping up and down. "But when will I meet her?"

"Next week," said the fortune-teller, "in biology class."

A policeman stops a drunk wandering the streets of Scunthorpe at four in the morning and says, "Can you explain why you are out at this hour, sir?"

The drunk replies, "If I was able to explain myself, I would have been home with the wife ages ago."

At a cricket match in Bourne, a fast bowler sent one down and it just clipped the bail. As nobody yelled "Ow's att", the batsman picked up the bail and replaced it. He looked at the umpire and said, "Windy today isn't it?"

"Yes," said the umpire, "Mind it doesn't blow your cap off when you're walking back to the pavilion."

A DEFRA Inspector goes to a small farm near Market Deeping and knocks the door of the humble, tied cottage. A young boy opens the door and asks what business the man has on his parent's property.

"I've come to inspect the farm for compliance with EU regulations, my boy. Where's your father?"

"You can't speak to him, he's busy," says the surly child.

"I shall speak to him. He's had notice of my visit," the Inspector retorted firmly.

"Well, he's feeding the pigs at the moment, "says the boy, "But you'll be able to tell me father easy enough - he's the one wearing a hat!"

One freezing cold December day, two blondes went for a walk in the Kesteven Forest in search of the perfect Christmas tree. Finally, after five hours looking, one turns to the other and says crossly, "That's it, I've had enough. I'm chopping down the next fir tree we see, whether it's decorated or not!"

A reporter from The Lincolnshire Echo was covering the Conference North Division Football League and went to see Boston United play Gainsborough Trinity. One of the Boston United players looked so old, he went over to him and said, "You know you might be the oldest man playing in the league. How do you do it at your age?"

The man replied, "I drink six pints every night, smoke two packets of fags a day, and eat tons of chips."

"Wow, that is incredible!" said the reporter, "How old did you say you were?"

"Twenty-two," said the player proudly.

A Stamford couple, Enid and Sidney, are having matrimonial difficulties and seek the advice of a counsellor. The couple are shown into a room where the counsellor asks Enid what problems, in her opinion, she faces in her relationship with Sidney.

"Well," she starts, "he shows me no affection, I don't seem to be important to him anymore. We don't share the same interests and I don't think he loves me at all." Enid has tears in her eyes as the counsellor walks over to her, gives her a big hug and kisses her firmly on the lips.

Sidney looks on in passive disbelief. The counsellor turns to Sidney and says, "This is what Enid needs once a day for the next month. Can you see that she gets it?"

Sidney looks unsettled, "Well I can drop her off everyday other than Wednesdays when I play snooker and Sundays when I go fishing!"

Two hawks were sitting on their perch at Woodside Falconry Park near Lincoln.

"Look at that speed!" said one hawk to another as the jet fighter plane hurtled over their heads towards RAF Scampton

"Hmph!" snorted the other. "You would fly as fast if your tail was on fire!"

What do you get if you cross the Leicester City with an OXO cube?

A laughing stock.

A man went to the doctor and said, "I've just been racing for the Scorpions on the Speedway track at Scunthorpe and I had a little spill. I thought nothing of it, but I got back home and I found that when I touched my legs, my arms, my head, and everywhere else, it really hurts."

After a careful examination the doctor concluded, "You have a broken finger."

A labourer in Boston, shouted up to his roofer mate on top of an old terraced house, saying, "Don't start climbing down this ladder, Bert."

"Why not?" Bert called back.

"Cos I moved it five minutes ago!" replied his mate.

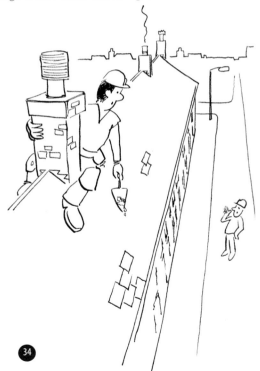

A police officer arrived at the scene of a major pile up on the M180.

The officer runs over to the front car and asks the driver, "Are you seriously hurt?"

The driver turns to the officer and says, "How should I know? Do I look like a lawyer?"

A blind bloke walks into a shop with his guide dog. He picks the dog up and starts swinging it around. Alarmed, a shop assistant calls out, "Can I help you, sir?'"

"No, thanks," says the blind bloke. "Just browsing."

One night an old couple in Holbeach were lying in bed. The husband was falling asleep but the wife was in a romantic mood and wanted to talk.

She said, "You used to hold my hand when we were courting."

Wearily he reached across, held her hand for a second and tried to get back to sleep.

A few moments later she said, "Then you used to kiss me."

Mildly irritated, he reached across, gave her a peck on the cheek and settled down to sleep.

Thirty seconds later she said, "Then you used to nibble my neck."

Angrily, he threw back the bedclothes and got out of bed.

"Where are you going?" she asked.

"To get my teeth!"

At a doctor's surgery in Saxilby, a patient was confiding in his G.P.

"Doctor, last night I made a Freudian slip. I was having dinner with my mother-in-law and wanted to say, 'Could you please pass the butter, ma.' But instead I said, 'You silly old cow, you've completely ruined my life and I can't stand the sight of your ugly mug'."

A bloke walked up to the foreman of a road laying gang in Grimsby and asked for a job. "I haven't got one for you today," said the foreman, looking up from his newspaper. "But if you walk half a mile down there, you'll find the gang and you can see if you like the work. I can put you on the list for tomorrow."

"That's great, mate," said the bloke as he wandered off down the road.

At the end of the shift, the man walked past the foreman and shouted, "Thanks, mate. See you in the morning."

The foreman looked up from his paper and called back, "You've enjoyed yourself then?"

"Yes, I have!" the bloke shouted, "But can I have a shovel or a pick to lean on like the rest of the gang tomorrow?"

A farmer was driving along a country road near the village of North Thoresby with a large load of fertiliser. A little boy, playing in front of his house, saw him and called out, "What do you have on your truck?"

"Fertiliser," the farmer replied.

"What are you going to do with it?" asked the little boy.

"Put it on strawberries," answered the farmer.

"You ought to live here," the little boy advised him. "We put sugar and cream on ours."

Sam worked in a telephone marketing company in Lincoln. One day he walked into his boss's office and said, "I'll be honest with you, I know the economy isn't great, but I have three companies after me, and, with respect, I would like to ask for a pay rise."

After a few minutes of haggling, his manager finally agreed to a 5% pay rise, and Sam happily got up to leave.

"By the way," asked the boss as Sam went to the door, "Which three companies are after you?"

"The electric company, the water company, and the phone company," Sam replied.

It was a quiet night in Bourne and a man and his wife were fast asleep, when there was an unexpected knock on the door. The man looked at his alarm clock. It was half past three in the morning. "I'm not getting out of bed at this time," he thought and rolled over.

There was another louder knock.

"Aren't you going to answer that?" asked his wife irritably.

So the man dragged himself out of bed and went downstairs. He opened the door to find a strange man standing outside. It didn't take the homeowner long to realise the man was drunk.

"Hi there," slurred the stranger. "Can you give me a push?"

"No, I'm sorry I most certainly can't. It's half past three in the morning and I was in bed," said the man and he slammed the front door.

He went back up to bed and told his wife what happened.

"That wasn't very nice of you," she said. "Remember that night we broke down in the pouring rain on the way to pick the kids up from the babysitter, and you had to knock on that man's door to get us started again? What would have happened if he'd told us to get lost?"

"But the man who just knocked on our door was drunk," replied her husband.

"Well, we can at least help move his car somewhere safe and sort him out a taxi," said his wife. "He needs our help."

So the husband got out of bed again, got dressed, and went downstairs. He opened the door, but couldn't to see the stranger anywhere so he shouted, "Hey, do you still want a push?"

In answer, he heard a voice call out, "Yes please!"

So, still unable to see the stranger, he shouted, "Where are you?"

"I'm over here, mate," the stranger replied, "on your swing."

For a minute Leicester City were in with a chance – then the game started.

The president of the Lincoln Vegetarian Society really couldn't control himself any more. He simply had to try some pork, just to see what it tasted like. So one day he told his members he was going away for a short break. He left town and headed to a restaurant in Swinderby. He sat down, ordered a roasted pig, and waited impatiently for his treat. After only a few minutes, he heard someone call his name, and, to his horror, he saw one of his members walking towards him. At exactly the same moment, the waiter arrived at his table, with a huge platter, holding a whole roasted pig with an apple in its mouth. "Isn't this place something?" said the president, thinking quickly, "Look at the way they serve apples!"

There was a fight in the Indian restaurant...the chef is in hospital in a korma!

Phil's nephew came to him with a problem. "I have my choice of two women," he said, with a worried frown, "A beautiful, penniless young girl whom I love dearly, and a rich widow who I don't really love."

"Follow your heart," Phil counselled, "marry the girl you love."

"Very well, Uncle Phil," said the nephew, "That's sound advice. Thank you."

"You're welcome," replied Phil with a smile, "By the way, where does the widow live?"

Did you hear about the magic tractor? It drove up the lane and turned into a field.

Three old boys, all a bit hard of hearing, were playing golf one fine day at the Horncastle Country Club.

One remarked to the other, "Windy, isn't it?"

"No," the second man replied, "It's Thursday…"

"So am I," chimed in the third man, "Let's have a beer."

At a school in Birchwood, the maths teacher poses a question to little Lee, "If I give £500 to your dad on 12% interest per annum, what will I get back after two years."

"Nothing," says Lee.

"I am afraid you know nothing about maths, Lee," says the teacher crossly.

"I am afraid too, sir," replies Lee, "You know nothing about my father."

A passenger in a taxi tapped the driver on the shoulder to ask him something.

The driver screamed, lost control of the cab, nearly hit a bus, drove upover the curb and stopped just inches from a large plate glass window.

For a few moments everything was silent in the cab, then the driver said, "Please, don't ever do that again. You scared the daylights out of me."

The passenger, who was also frightened, apologised and said he didn'trealise that a tap on the shoulder could frighten him so much, to which the

driver replied, "I'm sorry, it's really not your fault at all. Today is myfirst day driving a cab. I've been driving a hearse for the last twenty-five years."

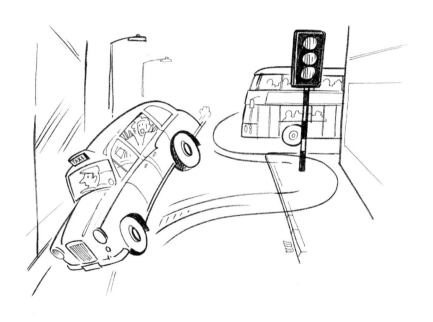

A high-rise building was going up in Grimsby and three steel erectors sat on a girder having their lunch.

"Oh, no, not cheese and pickle again," said Jim, the first one, "If I get the same again tomorrow, I'll jump off the girder.'

Harry opened his packet. "Oh, no, not a chicken salad with mayo and lettuce on granary," he said. "If I get the same again tomorrow, I'll jump off too."

Owen, the third man, opened his lunch. "Oh, no, not another potato sandwich," he said. "If I get the same again tomorrow, I'll follow you two off the girder."

The next day, Jim got cheese and pickle. Without delay, he jumped. Harry saw he had chicken salad with mayo and lettuce on granary, and with a wild cry, he leapt too. Then the third man,

Owen, opened his lunchbox. "Oh, no," he said. "Potato sandwiches." And he too jumped.

The foreman, who had overheard their conversation, reported what had happened, and the funerals were held together.

"If only I'd known," sobbed Jim's wife.

"If only he'd said," wailed Harry's wife.

"I don't understand it at all," said Owen's wife. "He always got his own sandwiches ready."

I had a car accident with a Magician - he came out of nowhere.

A farmer from Melton Mowbray once visited a farmer based near Long Bennington. The visitor asked, "How big is your farm?" to which the Lincolnshire farmer replied, "Can you see those trees over there? That's the boundary of my farmland."

"Is that all?" said the Leicestershire farmer, "It takes me three days to drive to the boundary of my farm."

The Long Bennington man looked at him and said, "I had a car like that once."

The nervous young batsman playing for Grantham was having a very bad day. In a quiet moment in the game, he muttered to the one of his team mates, "Well, I suppose you've seen worse players."

There was no response...so he said it again, "I said 'I guess you've seen worse players'."

His team mate looked at him and answered, "I heard you the first time. I was just trying to think..."

At a pub in Louth, a newcomer asked a local man, "Have you lived here all your life?"

The old man took a sip of his ale and, after a long pause, replied, "Don't know yet!"

A man rushed into Boston Pilgrim Hospital and asked a nurse for a cure for hiccups. Grabbing a cup of water, the nurse quickly splashed it into the man's face.

"What did you that for?" screamed the man, wiping his face.

"Well, you don't have the hiccups now, do you?" said the nurse.

"No," replied the man. "But my wife out in the car does."

A pupil at a school in Sutton Bridge asked his teacher, "Are 'trousers' singular or plural?"

The teacher replied, "They're singular on top and plural on the bottom."

A woman from Tetney called Tina was still not married at thirty-five and she was getting really tired of going to family weddings especially because her old Aunt Maud always came over and said, "You're next!"

It made Tina so annoyed, she racked her brains to figure out how to get Aunt Maud to stop. Sadly, an old uncle died and there was a big family funeral. Tina spotted Aunt Maud in the crematorium, walked over, pointed at the coffin and said, with a big smile, "You're next!"

The horse I bet on was so slow, the jockey kept a diary of the trip.

Peter walked up to the sales lady in the clothing department of a large shop in Grimsby.

"I would like to buy my wife a pretty pair of tights," he said. "Something cute with love-hearts or flower patterns."

"Oh, that's so sweet," exclaimed the sales lady, "I'll bet she'll be really surprised."

"I'll say," said Peter, "she's expecting a new diamond ring!"

Q: What do you do when a Leicester City fan throws a pin at you?

A: Run like mad, he's got a grenade in his mouth.

One day at Princess Diana Hospital in Lincoln, a group of primary school children were being given a tour. A nurse showed them the x-ray machines and asked them if they had ever had broke a bone.

One little boy raised his hand, "I did!"

"Did it hurt?" the nurse asked.

"No!" he replied.

"Wow, you must be a very brave boy!" said the nurse. "What did you break?"

"My sister's arm!"

A man and his wife walked past a swanky new restaurant in Grantham. "Did you smell that food?" the woman asked. "Wonderful!"

Being the kind-hearted, generous man that he was, her husband thought,

"What the heck, I'll treat her!"

So they walked past it a second time.

Scunthorpe United five – Leicester City nothing; they were lucky to get nothing.

Many years ago there was a dispute between two villages, one in Lincolnshire and the other in Leicestershire. One day the villagers heard the cry, "One man from Lincolnshire is stronger than one hundred Leicestershire men."

The villagers in Leicestershire were furious and immediately sent their hundred strongest men to engage with the enemy. They listened, horrified by the screams and shouts. After hours of fighting, all was quiet but none of the men returned.

Later on, the same voice shouted out, "Is that the best you can do?"

This fired up the people from Leicestershire and they rallied round, getting a thousand men to do battle. After days of the most frightful blood-curdling sounds, one man emerged from the battlefield, barely able to speak, but with his last breath he managed to murmur, "It's a trap, there's two of them!"

Did you hear about the truck driver from Grimsby who was seen desperately chiselling away at the brickwork after his lorry became stuck at the entrance to a tunnel?

"Why don't you let some air out of your tyres?" asked a helpful passer-by.

"No, mate," replied the driver, "It's the roof that won't go under, not the wheels."

BEWARE LOW BRIDGE!

Did you hear about the last wish of the henpecked husband of a house-proud wife?

He asked to have his ashes scattered on the carpet.

Pete and Larry hadn't seen each other in many years. They were having a long chat, telling each other all about their lives. Finally Pete invited Larry to visit him in his new flat in Mablethorpe. "I have a wife and three kids and I'd love to have you visit us."

"Great. Where do you live?"

"Here's the address. There's plenty of parking behind the flat. Park and come around to the front door, kick it open with your foot, go to the lift and press the button with your left elbow, then enter! When you reach the sixth floor, go down the hall until you see my name on the door. Then press the doorbell with your right elbow and I'll let you in."

"Great. But tell me...what is all this business of kicking the front door open, then pressing elevator buttons with my right, then my left elbow?"

Pete answered, "Surely you're not coming empty-handed?"

A man's car stalls on a country road near Coningsby. When he gets out to fix it, a horse in the nearby field comes up alongside the fence and leans over.

"Your trouble is probably with the injectors," says the horse.

Startled, the man jumps back and runs down the road until he meets a farmer. He tells the farmer his story.

"Was it a large white horse with a black mark over the right eye?" asks the farmer.

"Yes, yes," the agitated man replies.

"Oh, I wouldn't listen to her," says the farmer, "she doesn't know anything about cars."

One day a Leicestershire boy was in the back garden shouting,

"Mum, why is my Leicester Foxes top lying on the grass?"

His Mum looked out the window and shouted,

"The thieving gits stole my pegs!"

Have you heard about the latest machine in the arcade on Skegness Pier?

You put ten pence in and ask it any question and it gives you a true answer.

One visitor from Leicester tried it last week.

He asked the machine "Where is my father?"

The machine replied: "Your father is fishing in Kegworth." (Can you fish near Kegworth)

"Well," he thought, "That's daft for a start because my father is dead."

Next he asked, "Where is my mother's husband?"

The reply came back, "Your mother's husband is buried in Ashby-de-la-Zouch, but your father is still fishing in Kegworth."

"You're looking glum," the captain of Sleaford remarked to one of his players.

"Yes, the doctor says I can't play cricket," said the downcast man.

"Really?" replied the captain, "I didn't know he'd ever seen you play?"

Anne and Matt, a Lincolnshire couple, went to the Revesby Country Fair and found a weighing scale that tells your fortune and weight.

"Hey, listen to this," said Matt, showing his wife a small white card. "It says I'm bright, energetic, and a great husband."

"Yeah," Anna said, "And it has your weight wrong too."

Did you hear about the fight in the chip shop last week? Six fish got battered!

Supporters, waiting to watch Scunthorpe United play Leicester City, heard that the Leicester City players were going to be delayed.

They saw a sign on the A46 that said "Clean Lavatories"... so they did.

A man from Caistor decided to become a monk so he went to the monastery and talked to the head monk. The head monk said, "You must take a vow of silence and can only say two words every three years."

The man agreed and after the first three years, the head monk came to him and said, "What are your two words?"

"Food cold!" the man replied.

Three more years went by and the head monk came to him and said, "What are your two words?"

"Robe dirty!" the man exclaimed.

Three more years went by and the head monk came to him and said, "What are your two words?"

"I quit!" said the man.

"Well," the head monk replied, "I'm not surprised. You've done nothing but complain ever since you got here!"

There were two fish in a tank, one says, "You man the guns, I'll drive."

When the manager of Leicester City started to tell the team about tactics, half the players thought he was talking about a new kind of peppermint.

Two blokes are standing in the Grimsby Job Centre, waiting for their turn at the counter.

The first bloke says to the second one, "I have to buy my wife something nice for our wedding anniversary and the benefits cheque won't cover it."

The second bloke looks up from his paper and says, "What date?"

The first bloke thinks for a while and says, "15th September."

The second bloke considers his next question. "What year?"

Without taking a breath, the first bloke replies, "Every year for the last twenty-seven!"

A Hurrah Henry from Leicestershire was driving around Stamford in his fancy new car and realised that he was lost. The driver stopped a local character, old Tom, and said, "Hey, you there! Old man, what happens if I turn left here?"

"Don't know sir," replied Tom.

"Well, what if I turn right here - where will that take me?" continued the visitor.

"Don't know, sir," replied old Tom.

Becoming exasperated, the driver continued, "Well, what if I go straight on?"

A flicker of knowledge passed over old Tom's face but then he replied, "Don't know, sir."

"I say old man you don't know a lot do you?" retorted the posh bloke.

Old Tom looked at him and said, "I may not know a lot, sir, but I ain't lost like what you are!" With that, old Tom walked off leaving the motorist stranded.

Down the Nag's Head, a group of blokes sit around drinking when a mobile phone on the table rings. One of the men picks up the mobile and puts the speaker-phone on.

A woman's voice says, "How are you, darling? I hope you don't mind but I've just seen a diamond ring priced £2000 and wondered if I can buy it? I've got your credit card with me."

"Of course, my dear, go ahead," answers the man.

"While I'm on," purrs the lady, "I've noticed a top of the range car I'd like. It's only £65,000, could I order that as well?"

"Of course, my angel," replies the man.

His friends around the table look at each other in disbelief as the lady continues, "And I've just noticed a house on the coast, lover. It's only £750,000 - could we have that as well please?"

"Of course, sugar," answers the man, without so much as blinking.

The phone call is ended and the man smiles at the others and takes a long swill of beer. Then he looks around and shouts "Anyone know whose phone this is?"

There's a man in Coalville who claims to have invented a game that's a bit like cricket; what he doesn't realise is Leicestershire County Cricket Club's been playing it for years.

One winter's night, a lorry is going along the road near Harlaxton when the car behind, driving in from Leicestershire, starts flashing its headlights and sounding its horn. This goes on for a good ten minutes before the car finally overtakes the lorry on the dual carriageway and as it does so the driver, who is from Loughborough, rolls the window down and shouts to the lorry driver, "Hey, you! Don't you realise you're losing your load off the back?"

"I blooming well hope so!" The lorry driver shouts back. "I'm gritting the roads, ain't I!?"

An old bloke at the bus stop outside Scunthorpe General Hospital is talking to the next person in the queue whilst rubbing his head.

"My wooden leg ain't half giving me some gyp," complained the old boy.

The person in the queue looks at him, wondering why he keeps rubbing his head, and says, "Really? Why?"

The old man retorted, "Cos my missus keeps hitting me over the head with it!"

Two Sleaford Cricket Club players are chatting in the bar after a match. "So did you have a hard time explaining last week's game to the wife?" says one.

"I certainly did," says the other, "She found out I wasn't there!"

Three Lincolnshire women are talking in a bar about a party they've been invited to.

The first one says, "We've got to all wear an item that matches something belonging to our husbands at this party, haven't we?"

"Yeah," said the other two, "But what?"

The first one continued, "Well, my husband's got black hair and I've got a little black dress I can diet into by then."

The second one says, "That's a good idea. My husband has got brown hair and I've got a brown dress I can diet into by then too."

The third one looks a bit hesitant and says, "I just need to go on a diet - my husband's bald!"

Three Lincolnshire women are talking in a bar about a party they've been invited to.

The first one says, "We've got to all wear an item that matches something belonging to our husbands at this party, haven't we?"

"Yeah," said the other two, "But what?"

The first one continued, "Well, my husband's got black hair and I've got a little black dress I can diet into by then."

The second one says, "That's a good idea. My husband has got brown hair and I've got a brown dress I can diet into by then too."

The third one looks a bit hesitant and says, "I just need to go on a diet - my husband's bald!"